RAISING BOYS IN
TODAY'S DIGITAL WORLD

Proven Positive Parenting Tips for Raising Respectful, Successful and Confident Boys

Bukky Ekine-Ogunlana

© Copyright Bukky Ekine-Ogunlana 2025 – All rights reserved.

The content contained within this book may not be reproduced, duplicated, or transmitted without direct written permission from the author or the publisher.

Under no circumstance will any blame or legal responsibility be held against the publisher, or author, for any damages, reparation, or monetary loss due to the information contained within this book. Either directly or indirectly. You are responsible for your own choices, actions, and results.

Legal Notice:

This book is copyright protected. This book is only for personal use. You cannot amend, distribute, sell, use, quote, or paraphrase any part, or the content within this book, without the consent of the author or publisher.

Disclaimer Notice:

Please note the information contained within this document is for educational and entertainment purposes only. All effort has been executed to present accurate, up-to-date, and reliable, complete information. No warranties of any kind are declared or implied. Readers acknowledge that the author is not engaging in the rendering of legal, financial, medical, or professional advice. The content within this book has been derived from various sources. Please consult a licensed professional before attempting any techniques outlined in this book

By reading this document, the reader agrees that under no circumstances is the author responsible for any losses, direct or indirect, which are incurred as a result of the use of the information contained within this document, including, but not limited to,—errors, omissions, or inaccuracies.

Published by

TCEC Publishing

TCEC HouseEngland, Great Britain.

Dedication

This book is dedicated to our three amazing children and all the beautiful children worldwide who have passed through the T.C.E.C 6-16 years program over the years. Thank you for the opportunity to serve you and invest in your colorful and bright future.

Table of Contents

Introduction *Raising Boys Who Stand Firm* 5

Chapter 1 *Understanding Their Brains & Hearts* 8

Chapter 2 *Core Values and Emotional Fluency* 14

Chapter 3 *Discipline with Love & Boundaries* 20

Chapter 4 *The Power of Presence Fathers and Male Mentors in Raising Boys (0–12 Years Old)* 25

Chapter 5 *Nurturing Boys Through Mentorship & Emotional Intelligence*.... 33

Chapter 6 *Raising Boys vs Girls - Without Stereotypes Shackles* 39

Chapter 7 *When It's Hard: ADHD, Defiance & Chaos* 45

Chapter 8 *Faith & Spiritual Rhythms* 50

Chapter 9 *Screens, Devices & Digital Discipline* 56

Chapter 10 *Friendship, Bullying & Social Growth* 63

Chapter 11 *Strengthening Identity with Heritage & Service* 71

Chapter 12 *The Joy of Raising Sons* 77

Chapter 13 *The Journey Between Dirt, Laughter, and Legacy* 81

Final Thoughts: *More Than Just Little Boys* 86

Please Leave a 1-click Review! 92

Conclusion Raising Boys with Purpose and Compassion......................93

Other Books You'll Love! 97

References... 101

Introduction
Raising Boys Who Stand Firm

"Whoever heeds discipline shows the way to life, but whoever ignores correction leads others astray." - **Proverbs 10:17**

Imagine crafting a yummy, spongy and delicious wedding cake: each layer built with accurate precision, each ingredient chosen with every care. It can't be rushed. It needs time to rise, structure to stand, and balance to delight. Only when complete does it serve its purpose—beautiful, strong, and ready to eat.

In much the same way, a boy isn't born with character—he's shaped. Layer by layer. Obedience. Respect. Courage. Compassion. Discipline. Faith. These aren't automatic; they're baked in through daily training, intentional connection, and consistent grace.

Why Obedience Still very much Matters

Scripture shows us that even great men began with simple, daily obedience at home:

- **Samuel** (1 Samuel 3) first submitted to Eli before he could recognize God's voice. That early obedience laid the foundation for his spiritual legacy.

- **Jonah** knew truth, but resisted surrender. His rebellion led to turmoil; his return to obedience led to destiny.

When children don't learn to respect loving authority in the home, no classroom rule or external system can form lasting character. That's like icing an unbaked cake—pretty on the outside but collapsing under pressure.

What We've Learned from Real Families

- One father noticed his bright, confident son was falling apart at home—talking back, ignoring rules. So he paused tutoring and focused on obedience training: greeting others with respect, responding the first time, listening with eye contact. The transformation wasn't overnight—but it was deep and lasting.

- A single mom, hopeful for her son's success, enrolled him in boarding school early. He did well academically, but emotionally drifted. Without daily connection and discipline at home, his respect for authority faded. No teacher could replace the slow, loving shaping that is needed only a parent can give that.

What You'll Find Inside

- **Biblical roots** that guide discipline with grace—not guilt.

- **Age-specific tools**: from toddler emotion check-ins to preteen heart talks.

- **Behavior strategies** that build trust—not just outward compliance.

- **Copyable stories**: how one mom brought peace into a chaotic home, and how one dad saw respect take root after changing his approach.

- **Real encouragement** for single parents, blended families, and tech-worn households.

This book isn't about being perfect. It's about being present with a son. At times, you'll read something that stings—because parenting is sacred, messy work. But don't let that discourage you at any point in time. Your honesty, your prayers, your persistent love—they are building more than childhood. They are shaping eternity.

You're not just surviving these years.

You're raising a man.

Let's begin—layer by layer—with truth, love, and purpose.

Chapter 1
Understanding Their Brains & Hearts

"Children are a heritage from the Lord, offspring a reward from him. Like arrows in the hands of a warrior are sons born in one's youth." — ***Psalm 127:3–5***

From Day One, Boys Are Built Differently—and That's a Good Thing

When a son arrives—tiny, trusting, full of possibility—it's more than a biological event. It's a **spiritual calling**. Scripture calls sons "arrows"—not accidents. Arrows are shaped intentionally, pointed purposefully, and released wisely. That's our parenting mission.

Yes, boys differ biologically. But beyond the physical, what shapes their lives most is the **culture we model**, the boundaries we set, and the heart connection we build. This chapter helps you lean into what really matters—**brain science, emotional rhythm, and faith-rooted identity**—to begin shaping boys who are not just strong, but steady.

What Makes a Boy? Beyond Biology

Culture loves to tell us: *"Boys will be boys."* But what that often means is: "Let them be rude. Let them bottle emotions. Let them escape responsibility."

That mindset stunts growth.

When boys are told that tears are weakness, or that aggression is natural manhood, we don't empower them—we **confuse them**. Instead of confidence, they grow up guarded. Instead of empathy, they develop emotional invisibility. But what if we reshaped the narrative?

Let's give our sons permission to be **brave and kind**, **strong and sensitive**, **leaders and listeners**—just like Jesus.

Obedience at Home: Where Character Begins

Before school, sports, or youth group—**home** is the first classroom of character.

Academic success without obedience is like decorating an unbaked cake. It looks good but crumbles under heat. Without respect, self-control, and listening, even the best education can't shape a whole man.

Biblical Anchor: Obedience Precedes Calling

Young Samuel didn't just "hear" God overnight (1 Samuel 3). First, he **learned to listen**—to Eli. His earthly obedience prepared him for spiritual revelation. Obedience isn't control—it's **calibration** for a greater calling.

Real Stories. Real Shaping.
"We Paused Tutoring to Build Respect"

Marcus, a father of three, noticed his eldest son, Ezra, was acing school but constantly interrupting, arguing, and dismissing family rules. "He was smart—but unkind," Marcus said. So, they made a bold move: paused tutoring and began a *Respect Reset*.

Daily Drills:
- Eye contact when spoken to
- Responding with "Yes, Dad" or "Yes, Ma'am"
- Serving a sibling once a day
- One "respect moment" at the dinner table

By week four, Ezra wasn't just compliant—he was confident, more emotionally stable, and kinder at school too. "He found peace in structure," Marcus said.

"Boarding School Fixed Grades—But Not His Heart"

Janelle, a single mom, sent her son Elijah to boarding school at age 9, hoping that rules would fix his defiance. Grades improved—but the phone calls became more cold, the hugs less warm. "I thought achievement would soften him," she shared. "But love and discipline at home were what he really needed."

Later, when Elijah returned home, they began regular "Respect Circles"—5-minute talks after dinner about one win and one area for growth. Slowly, trust and obedience began to rebuild.

The Screen Trap: Early Tech, Early Trouble

One overlooked challenge? **Screen exposure.**

Daniel, age 7, once joyful and curious, grew moody and detached. Hours of unsupervised tablet time were rewiring his brain—feeding anxiety and disconnection. His mom replaced evening screens with outdoor play and scheduled regular "Nature Time" with a mentor from the community. It wasn't easy—but three months later, Daniel was laughing again. Less anxious. More connected.

Delay social media. Prioritize real play. Plug them into mentors and dirt—not just devices.

Practical Obedience Tools That Work

Here's how to help obedience become a habit—not a power struggle:

Daily & Weekly Tools

- **Obedience Challenge:** Start each day with, "Let's find 5 ways to say 'Yes, Sir/Ma'am' today."

- **Monthly Respect Awards:** Celebrate small wins—"Listening Legend," "Helping Hands," or "Respect MVP."

- **Conversation Scripts:** *"When you said X, it hurt. Next time, try: 'I'm sorry; I'll do better.'"*

- **Service and Apology Project:** For disrespect, teach repair: write a note, help a neighbor, or clean up without being asked.

Emotional and Spiritual Growth by Age

Use this guide as a rhythm map—not a rulebook.

Ages 0–2: Build Trust Through Presence

- **Science Insight:** Babies thrive on predictable patterns.

- **Spiritual Habit:** Blessing songs (e.g., "Bless your hands to help today")

- **Story:** When Emma's son Leo resisted sleep, she simply whispered their blessing song. He relaxed, trusted the pattern, and drifted off—feeling safe and known.

Ages 3–5: Emotion and Story Connection

- **Tool:** Emotion Naming Games

- **Faith Link:** Connect feelings to Bible heroes—"David felt scared; God helped him be brave."

- **Drill:** "What made you happy/sad/mad this week?" Then pray together.

Ages 6–8: Identity and Action

- **Challenge:** Weekly Value Goal—"Show kindness to someone new."

- **Spiritual Match:** Joseph's responsibility, David's courage

- **Purpose Play:** Let roughhousing and building become character workouts—"You're strong **and** gentle."

Ages 9–12: Self-Awareness and Purpose

- **Reflection Sunday:** Journal one win, one struggle, one way they saw God move.
- **Mentorship:** Review with a parent, grandparent, or youth leader.
- **Spiritual Development:** Guide identity talks: "You're more than your talent—you're a man of truth."

Why Brain and Faith Shape Character Together

- **Emotion grows through structure and trust.** Predictable routines wire the brain for peace.
- **Reflection and mentorship form a moral compass.** Boys need space to process—and people to guide them.
- **Bible truths root identity.** Jesus was gentle, strong, truthful, and kind—boys can be, too.

Quick Guide: Emotional and Spiritual Anchors

Age	Emotional Anchor	Spiritual Habit
0–2	Predictable bedtime cues	Blessing songs + touch
3–5	Emotion-naming play	Weekly Feel–Faith talk
6–8	Values + action goals	Hero verse + journal
9–12	Reflective journaling	Mentor goal-setting check

Final Word to Parents

You're not aiming for perfection—you're laying **bricks of legacy**.

Each bedtime song, each values talk, each act of discipline wrapped in love are the hands that shape your arrow. Boys don't just grow up—they're **formed**. And in a world full of noise and confusion, your consistent presence becomes their true north.

You're not just raising a boy.

You're shaping a man of integrity, anchored in faith, capable of love, strength, and purpose.

Let's keep going—because in Chapter 2, we go deeper: **how to build value habits and raise emotionally fluent sons who lead with heart.**

Chapter 2
Core Values and Emotional Fluency

"The one who heeds discipline shows the way to life, but whoever ignores correction leads others astray." — **Proverbs 10:17**

Imagine planting an oak tree. The roots grow very deep before the leaves ever show. Your son is just like that—he may look fine on the outside, but if the roots of character and conviction aren't growing underneath, he won't stand tall when storms come.

Core values like **honesty, respect, empathy, courage, and love** are not simply nice traits. They are the **moral and spiritual scaffolding** that hold a boy upright—and make him a man of truth.

Inspired by Ancient Wisdom: How Israel Raised Men

In biblical Israel, **by age 12**, most Jewish boys had memorized and internalized the **Torah—the first five books of Moses**. This wasn't just religious tradition—it was identity formation.

At that age, they were examined by elders on their understanding. If they passed, they were celebrated with a rite of passage: **they were called "sons of the commandment" (Bar Mitzvah)—men, now accountable to the law of God.**

This wasn't about head knowledge. It was about **shaping a worldview**—teaching boys to **think God's thoughts**, **choose God's ways**, and carry His truth into every area of life.

As modern parents, we can take a cue from this rhythm. We don't need to replicate the ceremony—but we **can model the intention**: to anchor our sons in **Scripture, responsibility, and faithfulness**, starting early and repeating often.

Values Aren't Preached Into Boys. They're Modeled—Daily.

Children might not always obey what you say. But they will **become what you consistently do**.

When a boy sees a parent speak gently under stress, admit when they're wrong, or show up with courage—those patterns imprint deeper than any lecture.

Every story you tell. Every prayer you whisper. Every boundary you reinforce. It's shaping his internal compass.

Ten Core Values That Build Men of Integrity

These values, rooted in Scripture and modeled by biblical parents, are foundations you can build into your son—starting today.

1. Respect

Taught by: tone, eye contact, honoring elders *Story:* Caleb rolled his eyes at Grandma. His dad paused and said, "Let's try again—with your eyes and your heart." They practiced twice. Now Grandma says, "That boy listens with his whole face."

Biblical Parent Model: *Abraham taught Isaac to revere God even when the command was hard.* (Genesis 22)

2. Honesty

Taught by: confession and restoration *Story:* When Michael lied about breaking a glass, his mom sat beside him and said, "It's okay to mess up. It's not okay to hide." They cleaned it together. Now, he brings his mistakes—before he's asked.

Biblical Parent Model: *Jacob taught Judah honesty after years of deceit. Judah later confessed and saved his family.* (Genesis 44)

3. Accountability

Taught by: owning your own mistakes first *Story:* Anna snapped one morning. That night she said, "I was wrong. I yelled. I'm sorry." Her son teared up and whispered, "I get mad too." A new level of trust was born.

Biblical Parent Model: *David urged Solomon to obey fully—while pointing out his own failures as a warning.* (1 Kings 2:1–4)

4. Empathy

Taught by: role-play and asking deeper questions *Story:* Mason laughed when a friend tripped. His dad asked, "Has anyone ever laughed when you got hurt?" Mason nodded, quiet. "So how could we respond better next time?" That night, he made a card for his friend.

Biblical Parent Model: *Joseph forgave his brothers—with tears—after being sold by them. He felt their shame and covered it with grace.* (Genesis 45)

5. Patience

Taught by: slowing down and waiting well *Story:* Ezra wanted to open birthday gifts before guests arrived. His mom said, "We wait together—it shows honor." He fussed, then proudly waited. Later, he said, "That was kind of fun."

Biblical Parent Model: *Noah's sons waited and worked beside him for decades, trusting a promise no one else could see.* (Genesis 6–9)

6. Determination

Taught by: setting small goals and sticking with them *Story:* Isaiah struggled in math. His mom made a 10-minute daily plan. With a reward in sight, he pushed through. He didn't just pass—he learned to persevere.

Biblical Parent Model: *Nehemiah inspired fathers and sons to rebuild Jerusalem—even with enemies mocking them.* (Nehemiah 4)

7. Curiosity
Taught by: embracing questions, exploring together *Story:* Luca asked, "How do stars stay up?" His dad admitted, "I'm not sure—but let's learn together." That moment opened a door to science—and deeper conversations about God.

Biblical Parent Model: *Solomon asked for wisdom—not wealth. His curiosity shaped a kingdom.* (1 Kings 3:5–14)

8. Justice
Taught by: standing for right, even when it's small *Story:* Aiden's classmate was bullied. His dad asked, "How would Jesus respond?" Aiden stood beside the boy the next day. Courage began with a conversation.

Biblical Parent Model: *Boaz protected Ruth with kindness when others ignored her. His real example still echoes today as an example to follow.* (Ruth 2)

9. Courage
Taught by: encouraging bold choices *Story:* Elijah feared speaking in class. His dad said, "Courage is trying, even with the fear." Elijah spoke. His voice cracked. But everyone clapped.

Biblical Parent Model: *Moses trained Joshua to lead without fear—even when facing giants.* (Deuteronomy 31)

10. Love
Taught by: affection, words, and time *Story:* Every day after school, Daniel's dad says, "I love you. I'm proud of you. You're God's boy." One day, Daniel whispered it to himself before a test. He knew he was rooted in love.

Biblical Parent Model: *God said of Jesus: "This is my Son, whom I love."* (Matthew 3:17)

Practical Tools to Practice Core Values
Daily Tools

- **Respect Tracker:** "Did I say 'Yes, ma'am' or 'Yes, sir' five times today?"
- **Confession Prompt:** "What's one thing I need to be honest about?"
- **Empathy Game:** "What would I feel if…?"

Weekly Rhythms

- **Family Council Night:** Share highs/lows. Pray together.
- **Respect MVP:** Celebrate growth, not perfection.

Conversation Starters
- "How did that choice show (or miss) one of our family values?"
- "What's one thing you're proud of this week?"
- "Let's act it out—what would kindness look like instead?"

When You Don't Get It Right

Michael lost his job—and became bitter. His son mirrored it. After months of chaos, Michael humbled himself, got help, and began praying with his son each night. Slowly, his boy softened. Not through lectures—but by watching **repentance lived out**.

A Note from a Modern Dad: Stephen's Story

Stephen wasn't a preacher—but he was consistent. At 6:30 every morning, he and his son read one Proverb, prayed, and packed breakfast. By age 12, his son initiated it.

"Repetition is what forms the very roots," Stephen says. "Not deep theology. Just daily presence."

Quick Reference: Value-Building Tools

Value	Tool
Respect	Respect Challenge Card
Honesty	Confession + Restoration Ritual
Accountability	Family Council
Empathy	Emotion Role-Play
Patience	Waiting Reward Chart
Determination	Weekly Goal Tracker
Curiosity	Try-Something-New Box
Justice	Community Service Project
Courage	Courage Challenge of the Month
Love	Daily Affirmation Ritual

Final Word: You Are the Teacher

You may never sit your son before elders and declare him a man like in ancient Israel. But every time you model integrity, pray with him, and discipline with compassion—you are **forming a man of God**.

You don't need perfection. You need purpose, presence, and patience.

Because you're not just raising a boy. You're forming an arrow.

> *"Like arrows in the hands of a warrior are sons born in one's youth."* — **Psalm 127:4**

Chapter 3
Discipline with Love & Boundaries

Why This Matters
Discipline isn't about control—it's about shaping a son who loves well, obeys with integrity, and leads with character. When correction is very consistent, compassionate, and purpose-driven, it builds endurance, not resentment.

1. Grounding in Scripture & Love
- **Discipline out of Love** "My son, do not despise the Lord's discipline…" (Proverbs 3:11–12) reminds us that loving guidance builds maturity, not shame. Think of a parent correcting a toddler kindly—not to punish, but to protect.

- **Lead Without Provoking** Ephesians 6:4 teaches: "Fathers, do not provoke your children to anger, but nurture them in the Lord." Picture a calm father who listens first before correcting—making discipline relational, not authoritarian.

- **Firm Yet Gentle** Just like Jesus, correction should always come with warmth and clarity—not harshness. A mother who gently explains why stealing is wrong models both authority and empathy.

2. The Authoritative Parenting Model
- **Love + Limits** Research shows that the authoritative style—warm yet firm—produces children who are confident, cooperative, and resilient

    Imagine parents who set clear expectations but invite dialogue when mistakes happen. That balance helps boys internalise values rather than fear punishment.

- **Teach, Don't Shame** Use correction as redirection. Instead of "You're bad," offer, "That choice hurt others—here's a better way." Step-by-step: notice misbehavior → take a calm pause → explain the impact → suggest a better choice grounded in God's love.

3. Tools for Consistency & Clarity

Behavior Chart / Sticker Chart (Ages 2–6) Visual cues like a sticker every time they use "gentle hands" reinforce the behavior. Stickers reward consistency—not perfection.

Weekly Points/Reward Chart (Ages 6–9) Points earned for chores, acts of kindness or listening lead to small rewards. Gradually transition to internal satisfaction and pride.

Reflection Chart (Ages 9–12) Weekly check-ins ask:
- What value did you grow in?
- What needs attention?
- How could you repair any harm?
  This encourages accountability and honest real reflection.

Conversation Scripts (All Ages) Use prompts like: "What happened? How could you choose differently next time? How might God's love guide your response?" These scripts turn correction into dialogue and growth.

4. Faith Habits That Reinforce Boundaries

- **Prayer & Pause** Before speaking correction: breathe, pray, and ask for calm wisdom—not reaction.

- **Pair Behavior with Bible Stories**
    - Honesty + Jacob's deception
    - Obedience + Samuel's listening
    - These stories help your son connect values with real faith examples.

- **Affirm + Encourage** Even when correcting, say: "I correct you because I love you—I am not upset with you, just with the choice." It reassures that relationship remains unbroken.

5. Age-Based Boundaries in Practice
Ages 0–3 (Foundation):
- Use routines for meals, cleanup, bedtime.
- Stickers for saying "please" or gentle behavior.
- Calm, simple redirect: "We use gentle hands."

Ages 4–7 (Structure):
- Use points for chores, listening, manners.
- Consequence example: skip dessert or tech time.
- Reflection prompt: "What happened? What could be better next time?"

Ages 8–12 (Ownership):
- Start "Respect Check-ins" and reflection charts.
- Invite them to help set rules—ownership builds compliance.
- Mentor check-ins: grandparents or a youth leader celebrates progress and helps coach character.

6. Biblical Principles to Anchor Discipline
Step-by-step example for Ephesians 6:4:
1. Child breaks a rule.
2. Calmly gather conversation.

3. Ask what happened.
4. Pray for clarity.
5. Speak truth in love.
6. Suggest biblical alternative behavior.

Never provoke anger: If frustration rises—pause, step away, model calm. This shows your son how to respond under frustration.

Love plus limits: Discipline is a bridge to peace, not conflict. "Discipline your children, and they will give you peace" (Proverbs 29:17).

7. Compassion Over Shame
- Avoid shaming language or forcing public humiliation.
- After consequences, offer restorative options: apology note, helping a neighbor, restitution.
- Be consistent: both parents use the same language and approach—mixed messages confuse children.

8. Real-Life Story & Takeaway
Training Trust, Not Triggering Fear
A mother implemented nightly honesty reflection charts for her 9-year-old, instead of immediate loss of privileges. He recorded his truth and apology. Over weeks, he chose honesty more often—not from fear, but to rebuild trust. His mom praised sincere effort and helped him connect honesty with God's truth—not just rule-following.

Final Encouragement
Discipline isn't punishment—it's heart formation. When boundaries are taught with clarity and compassion, expectations with consistency and grace, and correction with faith, your son learns purpose—not just obedience.

Faithful consistency + grace-filled structure = long-term peace, purpose, and integrity.

In **Chapter 4**, you'll discover *The Power of Presence*—how fathers and male mentors speak deeply into a son's soul through everyday example.

Chapter 4
The Power of Presence
*Fathers and Male Mentors in Raising Boys
(0–12 Years Old)*

"Start children off on the way they should go, and even when they are old they will not turn from it."— **Proverbs 22:6**

Raising a boy without a father in the home can feel like walking a tightrope—balancing love, discipline, and faith with no safety net. It's a road filled with joy, heartbreak, breakthroughs, and deep questions. But take heart: God's design has always included community—fathers, mentors, spiritual leaders—who help build up the next generation of godly men.

In Scripture, we find a powerful pattern: boys shaped by the loving presence of godly men grow into courageous, faithful men. Let's explore how, at every age, intentional habits with deliberate mentorship can nurture boys into very strong, faith-filled young men—even when their path begins in a single-parent home.

Ages 0–2: Toddlers – Laying the Spiritual Foundation
Spiritual Habit:

Begin a short bedtime prayer: "God, thank You for today. Help me grow."

These early rhythms become anchors of security and trust.

Biblical Inspiration:
Think of Hannah and baby Samuel (1 Samuel 1). Her prayers laid the very groundwork long before he spoke his first words. When she dedicated him

to God, she trusted that even in her absence that God's presence would remain and keep him throughout his journey.

Mentorship Moment:
Even toddlers absorb much love through presence. Inviting a godly male figure—an uncle, a friend, a pastor—to join in play or storytime.

Real Story:
Joanne, a single mum, regularly and deliberately invited her pastor and close male friends over for breakfast with her toddler, Liam. They played cars, read stories, and prayed before eating. Liam didn't just see men—he saw godly men vividly display a character that he could model.

The Heart Behind It:
Picture little Liam giggling as one of the men lifts him high in the air. Later, they pause to pray. That moment spoke louder than a sermon. "This is what love looks like." Though Liam's father wasn't there, love showed up anyway to him, it made his day and that stuck in his memory.

Ages 3—5: Preschool — Growing Gratitude and Boundaries

Spiritual Habit:
Start a "thankful talk" at dinner:

"What big thing did God do for you today?"

This simple ritual helps boys see God in their daily lives and they relate with him.

Biblical Inspiration:
Abraham's faith shaped Isaac—not just by words, but by action (Genesis 22). Gratitude and obedience go hand in hand when kids see faith lived out.

Mentorship Moment:
Create space for regular male-led faith moments—like Saturday mornings with a godly uncle, family friend, or men's group.

Real Story:
Sarah organized "Book Dates" for her preschooler David and her brother. They'd read Bible stories together, ask questions, related it to their daily activities and talk about Jesus while snacking on toast and fruit.

The Heart Behind It:
One day, David had a full-blown meltdown over sharing a toy truck, gripped tightly in his hands, became the battleground. His face flushed, tears streaming, he shouted, "It's mine!" and pushed his cousin away. His uncle **knelt gently** beside him, meeting his eye without judgment, and said softly, "Remember Isaac? He trusted God even when things were hard." That small moment didn't just correct his behavior. It shaped David's heart with grace.

Ages 6–8: Early Primary – Embedding Values and Emotional Strength

Spiritual Habit:
Start the day with a simple "Power Verse", like Proverbs 22:6 which is spoken together over breakfast or on the drive to school. Follow it with a short prayer, just a few honest words to invite God into the day.

Biblical Inspiration:
Jacob gave his son Joseph a powerful identity through blessing and love, even in a family full of tension (Genesis 37). Boys this age crave purpose and praise. They're forming their emotional and spiritual muscle.

Mentorship Moment:
Have regular "mentor meals", invite a trusted man to share meals where stories, faith, and fun mix naturally.

Real Story:
Michelle's son Luke joined a boys' group led by a kind, prayerful mentor. They visited seniors, made cards, and prayed together.

The Heart Behind It:
Luke's mentor once told the story of young David protecting his sheep (1 Samuel 17). That week, Luke helped an older lady with her shopping, then told his mum, "I was brave, like David." He felt strong—not because he was tough, but because he chose to serve.

Cautionary Example:
Julie noticed her son Mark becoming harsh and disrespectful. Without male role models, Mark copied what he saw online. He needed a visual aid to see how not to be disrespectful. His mum was now very deliberate to change and turn things wound by starting praying with him, teaching deep breathing, and reading and watching stories of biblical boys, his tone began to change.

Ages 9–12: Middle Primary – Building Identity, Purpose, and Resilience

Spiritual Habit:
Introduce a simple faith journal:

Encourage your son to jot down three simple things each day: one thing he's thankful for, one thing that was hard, and one small goal for tomorrow. It doesn't need to be perfect, it just need to be honest. This quiet rhythm helps him to name his feelings, reflect on his day, and see where God is at work. Over time, it builds more than just self-awareness—it roots him in faith.

Biblical Inspiration:
By the age of 12, Jewish boys were already being shaped for manhood, learning Scripture, asking big questions, and growing into their own faith. Even Jesus, at that age, did sat among the temple teachers, listening

intently, asking questions, and amazing them with His understanding (Luke 2:41–52). That wasn't a throwaway phase, it was a sacred season. These middle years, often overlooked, are full of potential. They're not just the "in-between" of childhood and adolescence—they're holy ground where deep spiritual roots can take hold.

Mentorship Moment:
Schedule "life check-ins" with a godly mentor — or you, as mum—using biblical heroes as conversation starters.

Real Story:
Liam, now older, faced a big test and was tempted to cheat. His mum reminded him of Joseph's integrity, even in Egypt. Liam made the honest choice and later said, "I feel like Joseph—free inside."

The Heart Behind It:
What helped Liam wasn't just the discipline, it was rather knowing that his story was part of something much bigger. He had men praying with him, speaking purpose over him, and a mother who modeled faith daily to him.

Cautionary Example:
A well-meaning dad focused only on grades and chores. His son did well in school but felt disconnected and unsure of who he was becoming. Without emotional or spiritual nurturing, his success felt hollow.

Hope for Single Mums
You don't have to do it all—but you **can** do the most important things:

Love deeply. Pray daily. Create rhythms. Invite trusted men to walk alongside you.

These years form your son's soul. With God's help—and the presence of godly mentors—you are building a man of strength, faith, and purpose.

"He will turn the hearts of the fathers to their children..."
Malachi 4:6

Summary: Single Parenthood Playbook by Age Group

Age	Focus	Key Activities & Biblical Model
0–2 Toddlers	Spiritual foundation	Bedtime prayer; Hannah and Samuel's dedication
3–5 Preschoolers	Gratitude and boundaries	Dinner gratitude chat; Abraham teaching Isaac obedience
6–8 Early Primary	Identity and emotional strength	Verse memorization; Jacob blessing Joseph
9–12 Middle Primary	Faith journaling and purpose	Torah memorization; Jesus at the temple

Key Tips for Single Parents

- **Quality over guilt:** Even a 15-minute mentor chat or simple prayer matters.

- **Build your village:** God's design includes mentors like Eli, who guided Samuel.

- **Lead with transparency:** Share your feelings honestly. Like David in the Psalms, show how to bring struggles to God.

- **Anchor in routine:** Spiritual and emotional disciplines mold identity, just as God's law shaped Israel's youth.

The Role of Fathers: Anchors in a Boy's Life
Fathers are often a child's first glimpse of what God's love and leadership can look like. Through their presence, they reflect both strength and tenderness—mirroring God's authority, yes, but also His deep care.

Emotional Anchors: A father's quiet strength during hard times—like Abraham trusting God, or Joseph staying faithful through trials—gives boys something solid to lean on.

Mentorship: Fathers don't just teach right from wrong; they show it, day by day. Their integrity, even in the little things, helps shape a boy's sense of what it means to be a man of character.

- **Quality Time:** Whether it's kicking a ball, fixing something together, or sharing a laugh, those simple moments create more than memories, they build trust, belonging, and connection that lasts a lifetime.

The Influence of Male Mentors
Mentors complement fathers. Examples include:

- **Eli and Samuel:** Eli mentored Samuel, guiding him to hear God's voice.

- **Uncles and family friends:** Like Moses raised by Pharaoh's daughter but mentored by Jethro.

Practical Steps for Fathers and Mentors
- Be present and intentional.
- Model Christlike behavior.
- Encourage independence and responsibility.
- Guide with love and patience.
- Celebrate achievements.

Reflecting on the Importance of Male Influence

The way you show up for your son—through love, correction, prayer, and presence—doesn't just impact today. It leaves a legacy. Long after you're gone, the strength of your character, the shape of your faith, and the way you treated others will echo in his life.

The Bible gives us a beautiful pattern of men like Abraham, Jacob, and David passing on faith and wisdom to the next generation. Your words, your habits, even your quiet sacrifices that are seeds planted in your son's heart that will bear fruit for years to come.

Your presence isn't just shaping his childhood. It's forming his identity and resilience in a way that can last a lifetime.

> *"Train up a child in the way he should go; even when he is old he will not depart from it."* — ***Proverbs 22:6***

Chapter 5
Nurturing Boys Through Mentorship & Emotional Intelligence

Great mentoring doesn't happen by accident. When spiritual, emotional, and creative support converge—from parents, fathers, or trusted male mentors—boys thrive. They become confident, kind, accountable, and resilient.

> *"Not many of you should become teachers...for you know we who teach will be judged more strictly."* — **James 3:1**

Underneath this warning is a life-giving invitation: mentor with care, heart, and intentionality. When mentors model values, offer emotional safety, and engage consistently, boys do better both at home and in the community.

Why Mentorship Matters
Boys thrive when they experience emotional security, spiritual modeling, and creative encouragement. Early positive intervention—especially in peer and spiritual groups—reduces aggression, disengagement, and disengaged behavior.

A Modern Story
Seven-year-old Marcus was angry and rude after leaving a single-parent home with little emotional support. Once he joined a weekly boys' group led by calm, faith-filled young men, he started to soften—sharing feelings, joining service projects, and channeling energy into purpose, not power.

Mentorship by Age (0–12 Years)

0–2 Toddlers

- **Spiritual Drill**: Toddler prayer song—"Thank You, God, for today."
- **Mentor Cue**: Invite a male mentor monthly for "story & prayer" visits.
- **Positive**: Joanne's son Liam baptized spiritual peace early through these short, gentle mentoring sessions.
- **Negative**: Maya's screen-only approach left her toddler defenseless to sudden routine changes—leading to frequent tantrums.
- **Tip**: Keep it light—two-minute gratitude bubbles at bedtime with a mentor figure bring emotional safety and relational trust.

3–5 Preschoolers

- **Spiritual Drill**: After dinner, ask: "What did God help you do today?"
- **Mentor Moment**: Monthly "Book & Prayer Date"—mentor reads a faith story and prays with mother + child.
- **Positive**: Sarah's son David learned creativity, compassion, and integrity through Saturday readings and prayers with his uncle.
- **Negative**: Lucy's child, left alone post-preschool with screens, developed aggressive behavior and emotional turbulence.
- **Tool**: Kindness Goal star chart—celebrate small wins and show how biblical values come alive.

6–8 Early Primary

- **Spiritual Drill**: Memorize and pronounce a Proverbs verse each morning, like Proverbs 22:6.

- **Mentor Rhythm**: Monthly mentor-meal includes verse discussion, prayer, and life-sharing.

- **Positive**: Luke, guided by a coach father figure, learned to serve seniors and grew in empathy and integrity.

- **Negative**: Mark insulted his teacher by age 7 due to lack of male guidance.

- **Biblical Model**: Consider **Joseph and his father Jacob**, who spoke blessings over Joseph—instilling identity, purpose, and emotional resilience (Genesis 37).

- **Structured Example**: At each mentor meeting:
    1. Start with shared meal and verse recitation.
    2. Ask gentle questions: "What did you see God do this week?"
    3. Plan a kindness or service action.
    4. End with prayer and a "Mentor & Me" badge—earned for verse, service, and character choice.

9–12 Middle Primary / Pre-Teen

- **Spiritual Drill**: Begin a simple "Faith Journal": 2 honest sentences each day—gratitude + one mistake.

- **Mentorship Flow**: Quarterly "Identity & Purpose Meeting" with mother or mentor.

- **Positive**: Joanne's Liam, through consistent journaling and mentoring, became a prefect known for integrity and spiritual depth.

- **Negative**: A single father who emphasized chores and academics saw his bright son grow disconnected—craving emotional and spiritual formation.

- **Biblical Model**: The **12-year-old Jesus** studying in the temple amazed elders and demonstrated the power of deep scriptural grounding (Luke 2:41–52).

- **Emotional Resilience Steps**:
    1. Begin each session sharing wins and struggles.
    2. Anchor conversation with a biblical hero (Joseph, David, Daniel).
    3. Pray together specifically for heart growth.

- **Tool**: Create a "Mentor-Approved Milestones" chart—values progress, journal entries, life lessons tied to biblical heroes.

Ingredients of Strong Mentorship

- **Consistency**: Regular, meaningful time together fosters trust.
- **Goal-Setting**: Mentors help boys dream with purpose.
- **Joy & Safety**: Fun, honest conversation builds emotional openness.
- **Parental Partnership**: Parents reinforce and support mentor lessons.
- **Recognition**: Celebrate achievements publicly or in prayer.

Mentorship at Home: You as Primary Mentor

You are your son's first mentor. You can model these behaviors even if no male mentor is available:

- **Self-Reliance**: Introduce chores, cooking, and independence from early age.
- **Choices & Consequences**: Let him pick clothes or activities with guided boundaries.

- **Quiet Routines**: Build calm 10-minute reading or drawing time to strengthen focus.

- **Impulse Control**: Teach "pause–breathe–talk" when emotions run high.

- **Conflict Resolution**: Focus on root causes and guide calm responses.

- **Honor & Respect**: Model respect toward women and elders. For example: Michael's son saw how calmly he spoke to his sister and apologized in front of her. That modeled respect and healthy emotional maturity in real time.

- **Emotional Growth over Grades**: Praise effort and character—not just academic success.

Building Emotional Intelligence (EI) in Boys

Emotional Intelligence is about recognizing, understanding, and managing emotions—your own and others'.

- **Emotional Vocabulary**: Teach feelings by using emotion charts or verbal naming during meals or bedtime.

- **Weekly Check-ins**: Ask, "What made you feel strong, sad, or proud today?"

- **Model Expressiveness**: Share your own age-appropriate emotions—"I felt worried today, but I prayed and let it go."

Techniques:

- **Active Listening**: Validate feelings when your boy expresses them.

- **Role-Playing**: Practice real-life scenarios ("What would you say if your friend dumped sand on you?")

- **Praise Emotional Effort**: Affirm when he expresses calm or honesty.

Final Thoughts

Mentoring is spiritual scaffolding. It's not a lecture—it's a rhythm of presence, values, conversation, and prayer. With mentors, even better. But even when it's just you, steady, intentional mentoring of your son helps him become grounded in character and emotionally resilient.

Whether through external mentors or your own hands, the goal is the same: **To raise sons who are confident lovers of God, anchored in virtue, and emotionally aware men of God.**

Chapter 6
Raising Boys vs Girls - Without Stereotypes Shackles

"Discipline your children, and they will give you peace; they will bring you the delights you desire." — Proverbs 29:17

From the moment he's born, your son is asking an invisible question:

"Am I safe to feel and be strong here?"
Many assume boys are naturally less emotional than girls. But studies show that **by age four**, boys and girls are equally capable of reading and expressing emotions. It's not biology that stunts a boy's emotional intelligence—it's **culture**. By age seven, many boys have already learned to bury their sadness, minimize fear, and trade vulnerability for performance.

But what if we, as parents, especially mothers, said: "No. Not here. In our home, emotion is strength. Tears are welcome. And manhood starts with love, not just rules."

That's what this chapter is about: helping you **raise a boy who knows how to feel, connect, obey, and lead with courage and compassion.**

The Boy Brain: What's Actually Different?
Boys' brains develop more slowly in areas related to **emotional regulation, verbal processing, and fine motor skills**. This means boys often:

- Struggle with patience
- Learn best by movement and doing
- Process emotion through **action**, not talk

That's why boys benefit from:
- **Delayed formal schooling**
- **Outdoor play and healthy risk**
- **Clear boundaries with loving connection**
- **Strong male mentors who model security and respect**

0–2 Years (Toddlers)
Emotion & Bonding

Boys desperately need touch, connection, and predictable affection. Physical bonding through hugs and rhythmic routines activates the parts of his brain that is responsible for **emotional regulation**.

Story:
Miriam, a first-time single mom, was worried she'd be "too soft." But every night she whispered the same prayer over Elijah during diaper time: **"God made you. He loves you. So do I."** By two, Elijah showed fewer tantrums and more emotional awareness than his peers.

Tips

- **Spiritual Drill**: Sing a God-verse like: "God made me, He loves me."

- **Mentor Cue**: A trusted male (uncle, pastor, friend) can offer simple play and prayer time monthly.

3–5 Years (Preschoolers)
Action = Emotion

Don't expect a boy to "talk it out." At this stage, he'll express fear, joy, or sadness through jumping, crashing, or laughing fits. That's normal. Girls may sit and talk; boys may need to move and act.

Real Life: Sandra used to think her son was being "bad" when he ran in circles after daycare. But after learning that action was emotional processing, she set up a "bounce and talk" station. He jumped on a mini-trampoline while she asked, "What did you feel today?"

Tools

- Ask: "What did you learn today?" Follow with: "And how did you feel doing it?"
- Balance attention if you have daughters who are more verbal—boys need emotional attunement too.
- **Spiritual Drill**: "Let's tell God what made us happy today."

6–8 Years (Early Primary)
Competitive, Group-Based Energy

Boys begin forming identity through **peer interaction**. They bond over games, structure, and accomplishment. These are your prime years to **plant spiritual values into action-based learning**.

Story:
Isaac, age 7, always played hard and loud. His mom struggled to connect with him until she joined him in a backyard football game, so she could just be present. Later that evening, he asked her to pray for his injured teammate. That night became the very start of their **"pray after play" tradition**.

Biblical Anchor:
David was mentored in courage and worship by his father and by Samuel. By age 12, he had cultivated a bold, emotional relationship with God through psalms and shepherding.

Tools
- Join his energy. Build with LEGO, race cars, or run.

- Afterward, do a spiritual anchor: "What's a verse about courage?"
- Discuss teamwork, fairness, and helping others.

9–12 Years (Preteen)
Emotional Growth Spurts

These years carry identity shifts. Boys face early puberty, changing voices, body insecurity, and emotional confusion—but often don't have words.

Story:
Every Thursday, Caleb and his mom made dinner together. One of the night he blurted out, "I feel like I don't fit in anywhere." She didn't fix it. She just said, "That's real, Caleb. Will you like to pray about it while we chop onions?" He nodded. It became their **onion prayer ritual**.

Biblical Parallel:
At **age 12**, **Jesus** was found in the temple, astonishing leaders with His questions (Luke 2:46–52). Jewish boys were expected to have learned the **Torah (Five Books of Moses)** by this age and be able to **defend their faith and identity**. This was emotional, spiritual, and intellectual initiation.

Tools

- Journaling: Two daily lines—"Today I felt..." and "Today I'm thankful for..."
- Spiritual Talk: "What do you think God is teaching you this week?"
- Practice confession and forgiveness.
- One-on-one drives, walks, or games create safe, non-pressured talk zones.

Spiritual Anchors: Stories That Shape Emotion

- **The Prodigal Father (Luke 15)**: Not just the son's mistake, but the father's emotionally vulnerable welcome teaches unconditional love.

- **Jesus blessing the children** (Mark 10:14): Dignity was given to the smallest, most ignored. Let your son see this gentleness.

- **Samuel's mother, Hannah**: She gave her son into God's hands, but not without daily prayer and emotional connection (1 Samuel 1).

How to Build Connection Through Habits
Weekly Rhythm Plan (Mother or Mentor):

Day	Habit	Emotional Focus
Monday	Morning verse & hug	Security
Wednesday	Ask: "What made you feel strong today?"	Confidence
Friday	One fun activity (sports, art)	Joy
Sunday	Share one mistake & prayer	Grace & Growth

Action Steps by Age

0–2:

- Hug and pray daily.
- Introduce a trusted male to play and read God-themed board books.

3–5:

- Play movement-based games together.
- Ask: "How did you feel today?" + Pray short bedtime prayers.

6–8:

- Join competitive play.

- Serve someone together: make cookies for a neighbor or sweep the porch for an elder.

9–12:
- One-on-one check-ins.
- Journal spiritual thoughts and feelings.
- Coach spiritual growth through identity talks, puberty hygiene conversations, and Scripture memory.

Final Thoughts: Balance the Wild and the Tender

Raising boys with discipline and emotional intelligence is like tuning a violin. Too tight, and you snap the string. Too loose, and it makes no sound. But tuned with **grace, structure, and spirit**, your son will sing with confidence, character, and compassion.

This chapter is not about making boys more like girls. It's about raising **boys to be whole**—wild in heart, strong in virtue, and secure in God.

Chapter 7
When It's Hard:
ADHD, Defiance & Chaos

Raising boys often feels like climbing a rugged hill—high energy, defiance, and endless days when nothing seems to settle. Yet even when chaos reigns, emotional and spiritual progress is possible.

When focus, kindness, and patience feel out of reach, spiritual rhythms and emotional frameworks—tailored for each age—help both you and him keep climbing toward hope and growth.

Ages 0–2: Toddlers—Energy Meets Emotion
Tiny boys test limits with boundless movement. But regular routines—especially short prayer songs and movement games—help channel their energy into calm.

Real Story:
Three-year-old Jamal would bounce on couches. His mom, desperate for peace, introduced a bedtime prayer song—"Jesus, make my body calm" sung during a quiet-down circle. Then they played "jump inside the lines" outdoors before sleep. Over weeks, Jamal shifted his energy to outdoor jumping and settled calmly each night.

Tool:
At bedtime, sing a short verse, affirm: "God made you brave," then hug and pray. This quiet ritual helps him transition from chaos to calm.

Ages 3–5: Preschool—Roughhousing Merged with Boundaries

These boys thrive in motion. Ask them to sit still, and they might melt down. The key is to pair fast movement with calm reflection.

Approach:
Offer high-energy "wild time" (10 minutes), followed by a quiet circle moment for listening lessons and a prayer walk—"God, help me listen... help me calm."

Biblical Anchor:
David, the shepherd boy, learned courage through physical risk (facing lions), then learned patience through his years at Saul's court (1 Samuel). Boys learn best when both body and heart are engaged.

Tool:
After active play, gather for a casual prayer walk, hug, and affirm your son's value—"God made you kind; thank you for trying."

Ages 6–8: Early Primary—Focus, Authority, and ADHD-Aware Tools

At this very age, energetic boys often collide with authority figures, especially if ADHD goes unrecognized. A child may struggle very much in class, feel judged, and stumble emotionally.

Positive Story:
Christian, age 7, disrupted class, frustrated with reading. A teacher suspected ADHD and with parents showed an angled approach: music during reading drills, breaks every 20 minutes, and reward charts for listening. Christian's confidence soared. He began reading in corners of the playground—proud and joyful.

Tool:
Use a "zone chart" for behavior—green (good listening), yellow (off-track), red (pause and calm). Pair it with a faith journal prompt: "Today I felt noisy, but tomorrow I'll try kindness." Review weekly and pray together: "God, help me listen and love."

Ages 9–12: Pre-Teen Identity, Impulse & Willpower

As boys grow, independence fights with authority. Screens become their safe zone—but often feed anxiety, loneliness, and superficial habits.

Story:

Malik, age 10, spent too much time gaming, growing isolated and restless. His mother replaced one hour of games per week with outdoor motorcycle outings and park visits. Over time, his mood lifted, his focus improved, and his curiosity for real-life experiences returned.

Tool:

Build a quarterly "Reflection & Values Tracker" with four parts:

1. Spiritual journal entry ("Today I saw God help me..."),
2. Mentor feedback,
3. Goal-setting for growth,
4. Challenge tied to a biblical hero (e.g. Daniel's courage or David's humility).

Biblical & Spiritual Anchors

Many boys feel pressure to be "tough." But the Bible shows many strong men who were deeply emotional:

- **David** wept over Saul even before reigning as king (1 Samuel 24).
- **Daniel** fasted and prayed in exile, modeling emotional and spiritual resilience.
- **Jesus** welcomed the children, wept over a fallen city, and wept at Lazarus's tomb (John 11): reminding us that strength and sensitivity coexist.

Daily rhythms—prayer, confession, gratitude—and relational check-ins carve direction when turbulence threatens.

Overwhelm Solutions (Ages 6–10): Step-by-Step Approach
When everything is going wrong...

1. **Pause the day**: Stop all activity. Breathe and pray: "God, calm our hearts."
2. **Emotion name**: "What's going on inside you right now?"
3. **Physical release**: Jump, run, punch pillows—but within agreed boundaries.
4. **Reflect**: "What made you mad/frustrated?"
5. **Anchor with Scripture**: Recite a short verse together (e.g. Psalm 46:10).
6. **Reset**: Offer a fresh chance. "Let's try kindness now." End with hug or prayer.

At-a-Glance Hill-Climbing Tips

Age Group	Tools & Rhythms
0–2	Prayer songs, routines, movement outlet
3–5	Structured wild play + prayer walks
6–8	ADHD-aware charts, faith journaling, verse memorization + reflection
9–12	Quarterly values tracker, outdoor risk/adventure, identity journals

Emotional Vocabulary and Intelligence
Effective Emotional Coaching involves daily practice:

- Use **emotion charts** with silly stickers to name feelings.
- Incorporate **dinner or bedtime check-ins**: "What felt strong, sad, or surprising today?"

- Model your own emotions: "I felt worried when I missed my bus—but I prayed and felt calm."

Interactive tools:
- **Role-play** funny scenarios: "If someone spilled juice on you, what might you feel and do?"
- **Celebrate emotional effort**: "I'm proud you said sorry after yelling."

Final Thoughts

Building emotional intelligence is not a side quest—it's the core of raising a well grounded, courageous son. It takes patience, laughter, tears, and prayer. With spiritual tools and emotional coaching, even the hardest climbs become moments of growth.

When your son learns to feel, reflect, and respond with courage and compassion—he doesn't just survive childhood. He becomes a man molded by God's kindness and strength.

Chapter 8
Faith & Spiritual Rhythms

Why Rhythm Matters

Faith isn't meant to be a one-time moment. It's a steady, growing part of life—like building muscle, it grows through small, repeated actions. Simple daily habits like prayer, scripture, reflection, and service don't just change behavior; they shape your child's heart, identity, and how they see the world.

This chapter is about building those **spiritual rhythms** into your day—not perfectly though, but regularly and meaningfully. Let's make faith part of your son's everyday story.

Morning Grace: Start the Day with Purpose

Create a simple loop each morning that sets your child's tone for the day.

Try This:
1. **Begin with a simple prayer** as you open the front door or buckle in the car:
   "God, guide my words and help me love well today."

2. **Ask a gratitude question** over breakfast:
   "What's one thing you're thankful for today?"
   Follow up: "How could you show your gratitude to someone else today?"

3. **Speak life into them** with a short blessing:
   "God made you kind and strong—live like that today."

Why it matters: This loop connects your child's identity to gratitude, love, and God's purpose—right from the start of their day.

Midweek Memory Verse Habit
Scripture doesn't need to be long or complicated. Repeating a single verse consistently builds truth into their heart and habits.

How to Do It:
- Pick one **simple verse** for the week that matches a value (e.g. Proverbs 10:17 – *"Whoever heeds discipline shows the way to life..."*)

- **Write it on the fridge**, a chalkboard, or near their play area.

- **Say it together** once a day—during breakfast or while playing.

- On **Sunday night**, ask:

  "What do you think this verse means?"
  "Did you see this truth happen in your week?"

Celebrate efforts, not just memorization. Use stickers, high fives, or just say, "I noticed how you lived out this verse!"

Evening Reflection Loop
Wind down with connection and meaning at bedtime. Just for about 5–10 minutes this helps build emotional awareness and a habit of grace.

Evening Questions:
1. **Emotion Check-In:**
   "What was your favorite part of today? What was hard?"

2. **Faith Moment:**
   "Where did you see God today?"
   "Did your memory verse help you today?"

3. **Repair and Grace:**
   "Is there anything you want to say sorry for—to God or someone else?"

Close with a short prayer. This rhythm helps your child process their day, say sorry, and rest with peace.

Mentor-Led Story Nights

Once a month, invite someone your child looks up to—an uncle, grandparent, coach, or youth leader—to share a Bible story and talk about what it means in real life.

How It Works:

- Mentor tells a story (5–10 min), linked to emotion or character:
  David & Goliath = Courage

  Jonah = Obedience after mistakes

- Ask your child:
  "What would you do in that story?"
  "How did God help?"

- Let them **draw a picture** or **write a sentence** about it.

- End with the mentor and parent **praying over that theme** for the child.

This helps your child see that faith isn't just for church—it's real, relational, and part of life.

Value Tracker & Habit Feedback

Use a simple dry-erase chart or app to track values your family is focusing on—like honesty, courage, or kindness.

Weekly Rhythm:
- List 2–3 values you're working on.
- Each week, your child marks:
  Green = "I did well"
  Yellow = "Still learning"
  Red = "Need to grow"

- Talk it through:
  "What helped this week?"
  "What could you try next week?"

Encourage effort, not perfection. The goal is growth, not performance.

Why Faith Rhythms Build Strong Hearts

- **Daily faith practices** give kids muscle memory for love, patience, honesty, and obedience.

- **Scripture and reflection** make faith practical—not just ideas, but tools for real life

- **Mentors** widen their faith world, showing them that faith is bigger than just family.

- **Evening check-ins** build emotional fluency and a safe space for grace.

Quick Reference Table

Time	Habit Loop	Purpose
Morning	Gratitude — Prayer — Blessing	Root identity in love and purpose
Midweek	Memory verse repetition	Embed God's truth in everyday choices
Monthly Mentor	Bible story — Discussion — Prayer	Build community + spiritual role modeling
Evening	Emotion check — Faith moment — Repair	Grow honesty, empathy, and spiritual maturity

Real Story: "Faith Loops Changed Our Chaos"

Theresa, a single mum, started daily loops with her 4-year-old son James. At first, bedtime was a battle. But after two weeks of:

- Mealtime reflection games ("What made God proud of you today?")
- Memory verse repetition
- Monthly mentoring by his uncle

James began to **choose kindness** on his own—sharing toys, speaking his verse aloud when frustrated. Bedtime became peaceful. Theresa said:

"Faith routines changed our emotional environment—and James began to own his behavior from kindness, not fear."

Parent Tip: Start Small

Don't try to do everything at once. Pick **one morning prayer** and **one evening reflection** to start. Once that's consistent, add the memory verse. Then bring in a mentor. Let the rhythm **grow naturally** until it becomes second nature—for both of you.

This chapter is all about helping your son grow into a young man whose faith is part of who he is—not just what he does. Small daily rhythms become lifelong anchors. And together, they'll help shape a heart that's strong, grounded, and open to God.

Chapter 9
Screens, Devices & Digital Discipline

Why This Chapter Matters

Screens are everywhere—at school, at home, and even in your pocket. For kids, they're fun, educational, and sometimes necessary. But **when screen time goes unchecked**, it begins to **disrupt sleep, fracture attention, shape values**, and even **disturb your child's spiritual rhythms**.

This chapter isn't about strict rules or counting screen hours—it's about helping your child **steward their attention** and use technology in ways that **honor God, build character**, and protect their well-being.

1. Biblical Foundations for Digital Discernment

1. *Steward Time Wisely* (Ephesians 5:15–16)
"Be careful how you live... making the most of every opportunity."

Think of your son's time like a jar. If screens fill up all the space, there's no room for play, prayer, or conversation.

Real story:
Anna noticed her 9-year-old, Micah, would go straight to the tablet after school with no conversation, no play. Just a scroll and snack. She introduced a simple rhythm: "Let's pause for 20 minutes when you get home—snack, tell me one thing about your day, then screens." That shift made space for real connection. Micah began sharing school joys—and worries—without a fight.

2. *Guard the Mind* (Philippians 4:8)
"Whatever is true, noble, pure... think about these things."

Media isn't neutral—it shapes how kids think and feel. Use Philippians as a filter for what your child watches.

Story:
After watching a funny show filled with sarcasm and insults, 7-year-old Caleb started snapping back at his little sister. His dad sat down with him and asked, "Would Jesus laugh at this too?" They swapped the show for a character-building cartoon, and Caleb's tone softened. They still laughed—but without learning meanness.

3. *Train Up, Not Let Loose* (Proverbs 22:6)
"Train up a child in the way he should go..."

Kids don't naturally know how to handle screens. They need guidance—not freedom to figure it out alone.

Story:
Maria set up a "tech talk" with her 11-year-old and framed it this way: "Part of growing up is learning to use devices wisely. I'll walk with you—not just say no." They made a family tech agreement together. It wasn't perfect—but it was a shared journey, not a battle.

2 What Science Says: Timing, Content & Consequences

Timing Matters More Than Minutes
Instead of tracking the very exact hours, look at *when* screens are used and *what* they replace.

Story:
Leo loved cartoons before bed. But after weeks of poor sleep and cranky mornings, his mom made a switch: screens off an hour before bedtime. They played Uno and prayed instead. Within a week, mornings improved, and Leo's mood shifted.

Sleep Disruption
Screens (especially blue light) suppress melatonin—causing later sleep and more restless nights.

Story:
Every night, 6-year-old Eli struggled to settle. Once his mom replaced tablet time with a bath and a book, his sleep deepened—and his behavior at school improved.

Brain Development & Behavior
- **Under 2 years**: More than 3 hours/day can delay speech and understanding.
- **Over 6 years**: More than 2 hours/day links to attention and impulse control issues.

Story:
When her toddler Lucy was getting moody and not speaking much, Karen cut down cartoons and increased reading and outdoor play. Within few months, Lucy's words bloomed, and her tantrums lessened.

3 Age-Appropriate Guidelines (with Christian Tech Covenants)

Age Screen Time Guidelines
0–18 months No screen time (except video calls)
18 months–5 yrs Max 1 hr/day of quality content, co-viewed
6–12 yrs 1–2 hrs/day max, focus on **context + content**

All ages No screens during meals or in bedrooms; stop screens 1 hour before bed

Content is King
Not all screen time is equal. Passive scrolling increases anxiety. But interactive, faith-filled or educational content, co-viewed with a parent, can be positive in small doses.

Story:
Jared swapped YouTube shorts for a nature show they watched together. "What does this show tell us about God's creativity?" his dad asked. Jared lit up—he was watching with meaning and curiosity

4 Faith-Driven Digital Disciplines

"Talk about them when you sit, walk, lie down, and rise up..."
– Deuteronomy 6:7

1. Perceive: Ask—*Is this screen time numbing or nourishing?*

Story:
After a 2-hour gaming session, 10-year-old Noah was wired and rude. His parents gently asked, "How do you feel right now?" He admitted: "Kind of grumpy." They began noticing patterns—and swapped long sessions for shorter, more intentional ones.

2. Align: Pick content that grows faith or character.

Story:
Instead of cartoons, 8-year-old Emma started watching Bible stories on RightNow Media. She began asking deeper questions at bedtime—faith was entering her very heart through her screen.

3. Set Boundaries: Create a Tech Covenant—a weekly Sunday check-in.
Include:
- Tech-free meals
- Sabbath blocks (e.g., Sunday afternoons screen-free)
- Consequences for breaking agreements

Story:
Every Sunday, the Thompsons ask: "How'd our screen week go?" No shame—just review, renew, and reset.

4. Teach Discernment
Help your child ask:
- "Why did I watch this?"
- "How did it make me feel?"
- "What would Jesus say about it ?"

Story:
After a superhero movie, Kai's dad asked, "What made that hero good?" That simple question sparked a great talk about strength and humility.

5. Open Communication
Ask weekly: "What's something you saw or played this week?"

Listen before reacting.

Story:
After her daughter admitted, she watched a scary clip at a sleepover, Sara stayed calm. "Thanks for telling me—let's talk about what to do next time." That built trust for future honesty.

6. Reclaim Sacred Time
Choose screen-free windows—like:
- Screenless Saturdays
- Device-free Sunday mornings
- Evenings for board games or family walks

Story:
The Johnsons declared Saturday mornings to "Tech-Free Adventure Time." One week, they baked. Another, they did built a fort. Their son said, "This is the best day!"—and screens weren't even missed.

5 Practical Tools & Family Rhythms

1. Create a Family Media Plan
Include:
- Shared family goals: honor, rest, spiritual growth
- Tech-free zones: bedrooms, dinner table
- Daily limits & Sabbath hours
- Built-in consequences

Story:
At a Sunday dinner, the Parkers wrote their plan on a poster. Their 9-year-old helped design it with stickers. When he hit his time limit later that week, he didn't complain—he had helped set the rule.

2. Model the Behavior

Story:
Every time Liam's dad picked up his phone, during dinner, Liam tuned out too. When Dad left it on the charger and made eye contact instead, dinner then became a space for laughter again.

3. Use Timers for Transitions

Story:
Instead of arguing over time, Maya's mom used a kitchen timer. "5 more minutes," she'd say. Maya knew the beep meant it was time to switch—and it worked with less pushback.

4. Co-View & Co-Reflect

Story:
After an animated movie, Sam's mom just asked, "What do you think God would say about that ending?" It became a habit—and screens became a place to practice faith-thinking.

5. Build Tech-Free Rituals
- Family game nights
- Nature walks with mentors
- No-phones-allowed meal prayers

Story:
Once a week, the Williams family did "Tech-Free Tuesday" with Bible trivia, popcorn, and a walk. Their boys began to *look forward* to it.

Why It's Worth the Effort
Without boundaries, screens replace real life: empathy, sleep, creativity, and faith all take a hit.

Story:
After tracking behavior for a month, Jenny noticed: on screen-heavy days, her son was more irritable, impatient, and distracted. On tech-light days? He was creative, cooperative, and curious. The data was undeniable.

But with rhythms and reflection, tech becomes a tool—not a trap. It can spark learning, deepen faith, and create connection—**when handled with care**.

Final Encouragement
Parenting in a digital world isn't very easy—but you don't have to fear screens. You're not just managing devices—you're **training hearts**. Every conversation, boundary, and shared moment sows seeds that grow into discernment, trust, and faith.

"Train them in the way they should go..."—and that includes how they hold a screen.

Next Up: Chapter 10 – Friendship, Bullying & Social Growth:

We'll explore how to help your son build healthy friendships, navigate peer pressure, and show courage and kindness in a complex social world.

Chapter 10
Friendship, Bullying & Social Growth

*"Armor of kindness, shield of wisdom,
community of encouragers."*

Friendship isn't just about having someone to play with—it's about **growing emotional strength, learning kindness**, and building a sense of belonging that helps your son thrive.

In this chapter, we'll explore how to help your child **navigate friendship, handle conflict**, stand strong against bullying, and develop the empathy and communication skills that create **lifelong social strength**.

1 Growing Sibling & Peer Empathy: Skills That Stick
Empathy is Learned

Empathy doesn't just "happen"—it's modeled. When your child sees you listening, apologizing, and considering others, they learn to do the same.

Illustration:
During a playdate, Max a 5-year-old did grab a toy from his friend. His dad knelt beside him and calmly said, "Max, look at his face. How do you think that made him to feel?" " Very sad," Max whispered. "What can we do?"

"Say sorry... and let him play too."

This brief pause trained Max to *see* someone else's emotions and respond with care.

Talk It Out – Role-Play Disagreements

Kids don't always know *how* to resolve a fight. Role-playing gives them a safe rehearsal space.

Step-by-step:
1. Ask your children to act out a disagreement (real or imagined).
2. Pause: "Now let's try again—can you express how you felt using words?"
3. Then switch roles: "What do *you* think your sibling was feeling?"
4. End with solution brainstorming: "What could you both try next time?"

Illustration:
When siblings Zoe and Liam kept fighting over who picks the movie, their mom said, "Let's act it out." They practiced calm words ("I feel left out") and tried "movie compromise night." The drama stopped—and respect grew.

Team-Up Projects

Working toward a shared goal teaches cooperation, patience, and appreciation for each other's gifts.

Try This:
- Build a LEGO world together with "team jobs."
- Plant a garden and assign roles: waterer, digger, seed dropper.
- Make a fort and plan who designs vs. decorates.

Illustration:
Building a birdhouse, 8-year-old Ben wanted to hammer everything. His little sister Emma held nails and painted. Their dad said, "Both jobs matter—without the holder, the hammer can't work." The message stuck very clearly.

2 Practical Tools for Caring Communication

Sibling Harmony Tools: Peace Kits
Make a "Peace Kit" together:
- Stress ball
- Emotion cards ("I feel frustrated...")
- Calm-down steps ("Breathe. Pause. Speak with kindness.")

Illustration:
After a meltdown, 6-year-old Levi went to the peace kit and picked the "I feel angry when..." card. His sister understood it wasn't just yelling—it was hurt. They worked through it calmly.

Peace Table Talks
When conflict runs high, use a "Peace Table."

How it works:
1. Sit at a table. One child speaks while the other listens.
2. No interrupting—use a "talking object" like a spoon or toy.
3. Reflect: "What did you hear your sibling say?"
4. Each offers a solution or apology—draw a picture, write a kind note, or hug it out.

Illustration:
After a shouting match, the Tran kids went to the peace table and sat down. With guidance, they each shared what was hurting each other. The result was lots of aplogies being shared, giggles, and warm handshake.

Cool-Down Zones
Create a cozy space with:
- Pillows
- Fidget toy or coloring book

- Deep-breathing poster

Let kids go here *before* resolving issues—so emotions don't explode mid-conversation.

Illustration:
When Mateo stomped off in frustration, his mom said, "Cool-down zone first, then we'll talk." Ten minutes later, he returned ready to explain—not explode.

3. Bullying & Peer Support: Practical Armor for Boys

Equip Them as Allies
Teach your son to notice exclusion or teasing—and gently speak up or include someone.

Step-by-step:
1. Practice phrases like: "That's not kind." / "You can sit with us."
2. Role-play scenarios during dinner.
3. Celebrate real examples from their life: "You stood up—that took courage!"

Illustration:
When his classmate was teased, 9-year-old Eli said, "Leave him alone." At home, his parents praised him very well: "That's what a real leader does." Eli stood taller that nigh.

Guide Peer Coaching
Help your son practice joining groups:

- Smile, walk up, and say: "Can I play too?"
- Practice tone and posture at home.

Illustration:
At the park, Nate hesitated at a soccer game. His dad whispered, "Use your line." Nate walked over and said, "Can I join?" They made room—and he made friends.

Talk About Media Moments
Watch shows or read books with characters facing exclusion.

Ask:
- "How did they feel?"
- "What would you have done?"
- "What would kindness look like here?"

Illustration:
After watching *Inside Out*, Ava said, "Sadness helped Riley be real." Her mom replied, "That's empathy—you saw someone's pain and didn't avoid it." A beautiful conversation followed.

4 Social Growth by Age: What They Need Most

Ages	Social Focus	Practical Tools
0–3	Sharing space, early turn-taking	Sing songs with turns, praise gentle behavior
3–6	Early friendships & big feelings	Read books on feelings, do puppet role-plays
7–9	Fairness, cooperation, group play	Chores as teams, "kindness points" at dinner
10–12	Loyalty, peer pressure navigation	Journal talks, mentor-led social reflections

5 Service, Rituals & Empathy Building

Weekly Kindness Circle
Once a week (Sunday night works well), go around and share:

- One kind thing someone did for you
- One kind thing you did for someone

Illustration:
At dinner, Luke said, "Ezra helped me clean Legos." Ezra beamed. Then his mom said, "I saw Luke let Ezra go first at the slide." The circle built gratitude and awareness of each other's kindness.

Service Builds Social Courage
Get involved in:
- Packing food boxes
- Making cards for elderly neighbors
- Picking up litter at the park

Step-by-step:
1. Pick a cause together,
2. Assign small roles: draw, pack, deliver.
3. Reflect afterward: "How did it feel to help?"

Illustration:
After serving cocoa at a winter shelter, 10-year-old Jay said, "They were so happy... and all I did was smile and pour!" He realized kindness isn't hard—it's powerful.

6 Why It All Matters: The Long View
Empathy Builds Resilience

Children who grow up learning how to connect emotionally are more likely to:
- Manage stress
- Build strong relationships
- Stay grounded in adversity

Illustration:
Tomas struggled with anxiety. But his parents focused on teaching him to name emotions and talk them through. Over time, his confidence grew—and so did his friendships.

Boys May Suffer More from Rejection
Research shows boys often internalize peer rejection more deeply—but having **a loving home base and emotional support** buffers the damage.

Illustration:
After being left out of a birthday party, Daniel was very crushed. His dad didn't rush to fix it. Instead, he listened, named the pain, and reminded Daniel of his worth. "You're more than one party—you're deeply loved." Daniel exhaled, and the tears softened.

7 What to Do Next

Host Sibling Mediation Nights
Once a week, set aside 15 minutes for kids to share anything lingering—listen, problem-solve, celebrate teamwork.

Practice Peer Role-Plays
Use pretend scenes:
- "What if your friend says something unkind?"
- "What if someone's being excluded—what can you do?"

Teach Emotional Coaching
After school, ask:
- "How did that feel?"
- "What could help next time?"
- Help them name emotions and think through their responses.

Final Word

Friendship, kindness, and conflict are not just part of childhood—they're a daily lab where your son is becoming someone others can trust, follow, and respect.

When you **model empathy**, teach gentle words, and encourage courage, you're not just helping your child "get along"—you're just shaping a boy who will carry **strength, compassion, and faith** into every relationship ahead.

Chapter 11
Strengthening Identity with Heritage & Service

"Rooted in the past, growing toward purpose."

There's something grounding about knowing *where you really come from*. Whether it's the smell of grandma's cooking, the story of a great-grandfather's courage, or a family tradition passed down with love— these are the very pieces that do form the foundation of your child's **identity**.

When your son feels connected to his family's story, values, and faith, he grows not just in confidence, but in **character and calling**. This chapter is about helping your child say, "I know who I am, and I know what I'm here to do."

1 The Power of Family Traditions
Family traditions are more than just fun, they're *anchors*. They give your child a rhythm, a sense of belonging, and a quiet message that you are *part of something meaningful*.

Illustration:
Every Friday night, the Thompson family lit a candle, said a prayer, and had "Gratitude Pizza Night." No screens was involved. Just stories, giggles, and shared slices. Ten years later, their grown up son said, "That's the time when I felt most like *us*. Very safe. Very much loved and Known."

Try This:
- Weekly "family dinner" with a special dessert or discussion question.
- Holiday rituals that include songs, blessings, or photo albums.
- Even simple routines—like "Sunday walks" or "birthday breakfast in bed"—can become identity-builders.

2 Storytelling: Connecting to Ancestry

Telling your child stories about where they come from is like handing them a torch—they carry that light with them.

Illustration:
When little Arlo asked about his middle name, his mom used the opportunity and told him about her grandfather, who once walked five miles daily to school. Arlo started saying, "I'm tough like Grandpa Joe." That small story really shaped his courage.

Try This:
- Share stories from your own childhood—the funny, the messy, the meaningful.
- Show photos, heirlooms, or cultural keepsakes. Talk about who they belonged to.
- Use bedtime or car rides for "heritage chats." Kids remember what's woven into quiet moments.

3 Service as Character Training

When kids serve, they begin to understand their power to make a difference. **Serving gives identity a purpose**.

Illustration:
9-year-old Elijah and his mom helped clean up trash at a local park. Afterward, he said, "I want to make our town nice all the time." That simple hour of service gave him pride and direction.

Try This:
- Help pack food boxes or deliver cards to seniors.
- Shovel a neighbor's driveway or bring soup to someone sick.
- Ask afterward: "How did that feel? What did you notice?"
- Reflection deepens the lesson.

4 Integrating Faith and Values

Faith practices does root your child in something deeper than emotions or the trends. They point to the truth, guide their choices, and shape who your son is becoming and will become when you are not present with him.

Illustration:
Each morning, Jamal and his mom made it a commitment and said a short prayer together: *"God, help me be kind and strong today."* One day after a tough moment at school, Jamal whispered to himself, *"God made me strong."* It stuck.

Try This:
- Morning or bedtime prayers with your child.

- Read a short Bible story and ask, "What does this show us about who we are?"

- Celebrate faith milestones: first communion, baptism, memorising a verse.

Faith isn't just instruction—it's **identity in motion**.

5 Celebrating Heritage

Celebrating your family's or community's cultural heritage gives your child **a sense of pride, perspective, and place**.

Illustration:

During New Year, Micah's family cooked traditional dishes, wore red, and shared why each greeting and symbol mattered. Micah said, "I love being part of this." The tradition reminded him of the fact that he *belongs here and he matters*.

Try This:

- Cook a traditional dish together and explain where it came from.

- Learn a song, dance, or craft from your culture—or from another to foster respect.

- Celebrate holidays together, to let your child experience the very *why* behind your traditions.

6 Practical Steps for Parents

Here's a guide that will help to help you build your child's sense of identity step by step:

Step	What to Do	Why It Matters
Create Family Culture	Weekly dinners, seasonal traditions, shared rituals	Builds belonging and continuity
Share Stories	Talk about your childhood, ancestors, funny moments	Connects child to a bigger story
Engage in Service	Volunteer together regularly	Grows compassion and character
Incorporate Faith	Prayer, Bible reflection, spiritual talks	Anchors identity in truth
Celebrate Heritage	Enjoy cultural food, dress, stories, and music	Cultivates pride and connection

Final Word: Why It All Matters

Your son is growing up in a world that's loud and often very confusing. But when you root him in **heritage, service, and faith**, you give him a map and a mirror.

He'll know:
- "This is where I come from and being able to relate with it."
- "This is what I stand for."
- "This is how I can help."

Final Illustration:

When a 12-year-old Julian, gave a speech at school about his great-grandmother's journey to freedom, he stood tall. "She was brave," he said.

"And I want to be brave too." His identity wasn't just shaped—it was **claimed because he knew**.

Coming Up: Chapter 12 – *The Joy of Raising Sons*
We'll shift from identity to the everyday joy of the parenting journey—how to emotionally connect with your boy, celebrate his growth, and enjoy the sacred, silly, and stretching moments of raising him well.

Chapter 12
The Joy of Raising Sons

"Nurturing hearts, shaping futures."

Raising boys isn't just about guiding their behavior—it's about shaping their very hearts. When you lean into everyday moments with connection, presence, and play, you don't just *raise a child*—you help build a strong, emotionally grounded man.

This chapter invites you to pause, laugh, listen—and lean into the joy of parenting with presence and purpose.

1 Daily Emotional Bonding: The Foundation of Connection
Your presence matters more than perfection. Boys might not always say it, but they crave emotional connection—and they learn how to express their inner world by watching you.

Story: "The Drive-Home Connection"
Every afternoon, Marcus would pick up his 9-year-old son, Eli, from school. At first, Eli gave one-word answers. But Marcus kept sharing *his* day: "I got frustrated at work today—had to take some deep breaths." Over time, Eli opened up too: "I got mad in PE today, but I tried your breathing trick."

That 15-minute drive became their emotional lifeline.

Try This:
- End the day with "highs and lows"—ask: *"What was the best and hardest part of your day?"*

- Use moments like dinner, drives, or bedtime to connect emotionally.
- Model emotional language: "I felt proud when you helped your sister today."

2 Father-Son Rituals: Building Traditions of Trust

Rituals don't have to be fancy—they just need to be consistent. A shared pancake breakfast on Saturdays, bedtime reading, or even fixing things together can become sacred ground for relationship-building.

Story: "The Saturday Toolbox"
Jared and his son Leo fixed something together every Saturday—leaky pipes, broken toys, old furniture. One Saturday, Leo asked, "Can we fix my feelings too?" That routine had built trust—and opened space for real talk.

Try This:
- Start a weekly "Dad & Me" outing: bike rides, board games, coffee dates.
- Build something together—a fort, model kit, or garden bed.
- End the day with a "Blessing Ritual": a short prayer, hug, or shared phrase like *"You're my brave boy."*

3 Gratitude Practices: Cultivating a Heart of Thankfulness

Gratitude doesn't just make kids happier—it helps them bounce back from hard things. It trains the heart to notice *what's good*, even in very hard seasons.

Story: "The Grateful Jar"
Every night before bed, 7-year-old Aiden and his mom each wrote one thing they were thankful for and dropped it in their "Thank You Jar." One tough week, Aiden read through past notes: "I still have a family who loves me." Gratitude gave him strength.

Try This:
- Create a "Gratitude Jar"—add one thankful note each evening.
- At dinner, go around and say one thing you're grateful for.
- Connect gratitude to God: *"Thank you, Lord, for this silly moment."*

4 Celebrating Growth: Recognizing Milestones and Efforts

Boys need to hear: *"I see how hard you're trying."* Focusing on growth, not just grades or goals, helps build internal motivation and a healthy view of success.

Story: "The 'You Did It' Wall"
After his son Jace learned to tie his shoes after months of trying, Chris taped the shoelaces on a wall and wrote, "You didn't quit." Soon the wall filled with moments: riding a bike, apologizing first, memorizing a verse. It wasn't about trophies—it was about effort.

Try This:
- Celebrate "small wins" with a note, sticker, or special snack.
- Create a "Wins Wall" or jar filled with little triumphs.
- Say: *"I'm proud of how you stuck with that—even when it was tough."*

5 Modeling Emotional Health: Leading by Example

Boys watch more than they listen. When you show them how you handle anger, sadness, or stress in healthy ways, they learn what strength looks like.

Story: "Dad Cried First"
One night, after a tough day, Ray told his son, "I'm feeling sad and tired—I need a hug." His son, surprised, wrapped him in one. Later, when the boy got overwhelmed at school, he said, "I need a hug like you did, Dad." That moment of vulnerability became his very model for strength.

Try This:
- Use emotion words in front of your son: "I'm feeling overwhelmed, so I'm taking a break."
- Share how you deal with big feelings—prayer, breathing, journaling.
- Normalize emotions: "It's okay to cry. It means your heart's working."

Final Word: The Gift of Raising Sons

Raising a boy is a front-row seat to transformation. One day he's laughing in the dirt, the next he's asking big questions about life and purpose. Every shared laugh, honest talk, and quiet prayer becomes part of his foundation.

Here's what your consistent love teaches him:
- *"I matter."*
- *"I can feel deeply and still be strong."*
- *"I have someone who sees me—and believes in me."*

Parenting sons is joyful, sometimes messy, always meaningful. You're not just raising a boy. You're raising someone's future protector, peacemaker, friend, father—and it all starts with your daily presence.

Next: Chapter 13 — *The Journey Between Dirt, Laughter & Legacy*

We'll wrap the series by reflecting on what it means to raise boys with an eye on eternity: shaping souls, not just behavior—and letting joy, service, and spiritual heritage guide the long journey ahead.

Chapter 13
The Journey Between Dirt, Laughter, and Legacy

Raising boys is like living with a sparkler—sometimes it burns, sometimes it lights the room. But if you stay close, you'll see the wonder. Amid the scraped knees, mess, and strong wills, there's joy—a deep soul-lifting joy—in watching a boy become a man of courage, compassion, and character.

This chapter is your breath of fresh air: not just tips, but moments of delight, purpose, and awe—even on the loudest, messiest days.

Ages 0–2: The Foundation of Wonder
The toddler years are filled with holy chaos: soggy onesies, endless motion, first words, and wide-eyed discovery. These are years where spiritual and emotional roots begin.

Real Joy
Three little words changed everything for young Isaiah's mom. Each night, she whispered during their bedtime routine:

"God made you."

Then she'd sing a short verse over him: *"You are fearfully and wonderfully made."*
In time, even when tantrums raged, Isaiah calmed at the familiar rhythm of that nightly blessing.

Tool: Milestone + Prayer Board
Create a visual memory board—"first smile," "first step," "first prayer"—and pair it with a blessing. Each milestone is marked with a whisper of God's love.

Spiritual Drill: End each day with a hug and say: "God made you strong. God made you loved."

Like Hannah offering Samuel (1 Samuel 1:27–28), your quiet rituals shape legacy.

Ages 3–5: Loud Love, Big Emotions

Preschoolers live in color. Joy pours from stick-figure drawings, mud puddles, and wild laughter. But so do tears, tantrums, and big feelings. These years lay the emotional groundwork for empathy, gratitude, and boundaries.

True Story – David & Gratitude

Five-year-old David was always in motion—shouting, climbing, tumbling. But every Thursday, his godfather came over for "Bible snack hour." They read one story, then drew what made them happy. Slowly, David began saying things like:

"God was happy I shared my blocks today."

Practical Tool: Talk & Pray Time

After playtime, wind down with three gentle questions:
1. What made you smile today?
2. What made God happy?
3. Who did you help?

Anchor this with a short prayer and a loving hug.

Emotional Cue: Use sticker charts for kindness. Celebrate emotional wins as much as behavior ones.

Biblical Parallel: Like young Samuel hearing God's voice in the night (1 Samuel 3), these moments train boys to listen—to themselves and to God.

Ages 6–8: Building Skills, Grit, and Emotional Muscles

These are the golden years of questions, courage, and quick growth. Boys develop hobbies and show bursts of emotional awareness. This is where spiritual values and emotional intelligence meet practice.

The "Value + Verse" Method

Each week, pick one virtue (e.g., courage, truth, patience), pair it with a Bible story (like Daniel in the lion's den for courage), and act it out or draw it.

Growth Tool:

- Set small weekly goals tied to values.
- End the week with a "joy circle": what he learned, how he helped, where he struggled.

Impulse & Social Skills Hack

For boys who struggle to wait their turn or handle disappointment, practice scenarios through play.

"Let's pretend your brother knocks over your blocks—what could you do instead of yelling?"

Model, laugh, repeat. Build emotional muscle like any other skill.

Jesus' Childhood: "And Jesus grew in wisdom and stature, and in favor with God and man" (Luke 2:52). Growth includes emotional and spiritual awareness.

Ages 9–12: Identity, Independence & Deeper Joy

These are the bridge years—no longer little, not yet teens. Boys begin testing limits, asking bigger questions, and wanting autonomy. Emotions deepen. Joy can be harder to spot—but richer when it's found.

Malik's Story – Choosing Connection

Malik, age 10, was slipping away into screen-time silence. One day, his mom proposed a trade:

"One hour of screens for one hike with me."

He agreed, half-hearted. But over months, that walk turned into a space of trust.

He talked more. Slept better and even Smiled again.

Action Tool: "No-Screen Zones" and Outdoor Connection Time
Replace some digital time with hikes, woodworking, bike rides, or even errands. Let him lead the conversation—or the direction.

Spiritual Rhythm: "Reflection Sundays"
Set aside time each week for:

- **Faith journal**: What did I learn about myself and God?
- **Mentor feedback** (could be dad, uncle, or spiritual leader)
- **Next week's goal**: tied to a Bible hero (e.g., Joseph's forgiveness, David's honesty)

Biblical Anchor: Jesus, even as a boy, knew his identity and purpose (Luke 2:49). Help your son ask: "What kind of man is God helping me become?"

Age-Grouped Summary: Joyful Faith Patterns

Age	Joy Practice
0–2	Bedtime verse + "God loves me" song, milestone prayer board, hugs & blessing
3–5	Nightly "What made God happy?" stories, walk-and-pray circles, sticker charts
6–8	Weekly value + Bible verse, spiritual mentor talks, kindness challenges
9–12	Reflection Sundays, goal journaling, reduced tech + adventure days

Final Thoughts:
More Than Just Little Boys

You're not just managing energy or correcting behavior—you're raising sons who will become men. Every bedtime song, every timeout followed by a hug, every morning devotional matters.

You are shaping tomorrow's protectors, preachers, inventors, teachers, fathers, and husbands. You are building men of legacy. And yes, the joy? It's found in the journey, not the destination.

> *"I have no greater joy than to hear that my children are walking in the truth."* —3 John 1:4

Take heart. You're not doing it alone—and every loving moment matters more than you'll ever know.

Appendix: Q&A with Parents — Common Challenges Answered

Real questions from real parents—answered with empathy, tools, and stories.

Parenting boys can be full of delight and mystery—one minute they're giving hugs, the next they're launching into chaos. Here are some of the most common parenting challenges, with down-to-earth, step-by-step advice (plus examples from families like yours).

Q1: How can I address nap resistance in toddlers?

Answer: Toddlers do thrive on routine and calm. When naps become a battle, the key is to turn nap time into a rhythm, not a command.

Story: "The Wind-Down Basket"

Leah's 2-year-old, Noah, would scream at the word *"nap."* So she created a "wind-down basket" with the same 3 things every day: a picture book, a soft blanket, and a lavender-scented plush toy. She dimmed the lights, sat with him, read the same story, then played soft music. After a few days, his body began to associate that rhythm with rest. He still resisted sometimes—but not with screaming. He had a ritual now, and rituals calm brains.

Steps:
1. **Pick a daily nap window** (same time each day).
2. **Create a pre-nap routine**: book, blanket, music, prayer.
3. **Control the environment**: quiet, dim, cool room.
4. **Stay calm and predictable**—consistency builds trust.
5. **Use a visual cue** (like a chart or sticker) to mark nap days.

Q2: My son is frequently defiant. How can I manage this behavior?

Answer: Defiance isn't just "bad behavior"—it's often a signal. Boys push boundaries to see where they end—and who still loves them when they cross them.

Story: "Power Through Partnership"
Six-year-old Jayden kept refusing to clean up after playtime. His mom, Alana, realized she was always shouting instructions from across the room. One day, she sat next to him and said, "You like being the leader, right?" He nodded. "Let's make a clean-up map. You lead, I'll follow." Jayden grinned—and began organizing. When she gave him just choices, like *"Do you want to clean blocks or books first?"*, the defiance softened. He felt seen, not just corrected.

Steps:
1. **Stay calm**—don't mirror the defiance.
2. **Offer choices** within limits: "You can brush teeth before or after PJs."

3. **Use clear, consistent rules** with predictable consequences.

4. **Validate emotion, hold the boundary**: "I know you're upset, but the rule stays the same."

5. **Praise cooperation**: "You chose to be kind today—that took strength!"

Q3: Tantrums seem to occur often. What strategies can help?

Answer: Tantrums are a child's way of saying, *"I'm overwhelmed, and I don't know what to do with this big feeling."* Calm, connection, and coaching help them build regulation skills.

Story: *"The Feelings Train"*

When 4-year-old Mateo screamed over a broken cracker, his dad would freeze. Then he started using a "Feelings Train" chart. Each train car had a feeling: mad, sad, excited, tired. During calm moments, they'd name feelings and act them out. When a tantrum hit, his dad pointed to the chart and said, "Which car are we in?" Mateo pointed to "mad." They'd take 5 breaths, then talk. It didn't stop tantrums—but it gave them both tools.

Steps:

1. **Stay near and calm**: "I'm here. You're safe."

2. **Use fewer words in the moment**—the brain is in meltdown mode.

3. **Afterwards, reflect**: "What happened? What helped you calm down?"

4. **Practice ahead of time**: role-play, use books about emotions.

5. **Teach coping tools**: breathing, stress balls, feelings charts.

Q4: My child has frequent tech meltdowns. How can I manage screen time very effectively?

Answer: Meltdowns around screens often reflect a lack of clarity or transition. Instead of just saying "time's up," teach them *when, how long,* and *what happens next.*

Story: "The Kitchen Timer Trick"
Ella set clear rules: no screens before breakfast or after dinner. But her son, Luca, would still melt down when time was up. So she introduced a kitchen timer and a "next activity board." Ten minutes before time was up, she'd say, "What will you do after screens—play blocks or color?" Giving a *next step* and a *warning* helped Luca feel more in control. The timer beeped—no debate, just transition.

Steps:
1. **Create a family tech plan**: clear rules for time/place.
2. **Use visual timers**: kitchen timers, sand timers, apps.
3. **Give a 10-minute warning** before transition.
4. **Offer a choice for what comes next**: "Screens are off. Want to ride your bike or read?"
5. **Praise calm transitions**—celebrate it!

Q5: My son has been diagnosed with ADHD. What strategies can support his development?

Answer: Boys with ADHD are wired for movement and spontaneity—but they thrive with structure, empathy, and small wins.

Story: "The Color Code Wall"
Eight-year-old Dax couldn't sit still and often forgot steps in routines. His mom made a color-coded wall chart: *Red = Morning jobs, Yellow = After school, Blue = Bedtime.* Each task had a visual icon. Dax raced to complete his "colors." She also gave "wiggle breaks" every 20 minutes.

With very clear structure, he went from daily meltdowns to self-starting routines.

Steps:
1. **Break tasks into steps** with pictures or colors.
2. **Use timers** for activities and transitions.
3. **Give movement breaks** often.
4. **Celebrate effort, not just results**: "You stayed focused for 10 minutes—awesome!"
5. **Work with teachers** to align strategies.

Q6: My son struggles with friendships. How can I support his social development?

Answer: Boys aren't always verbal about friendship struggles. But they long to belong. Your coaching and encouragement matter more than you think.

Story: "The Friendship Role-Play"
Logan struggled to make friends. His dad started role-playing social skills: how to ask to join a game, what to say when someone's sad. They practiced after dinner for 5 minutes. One day, Logan said, "I tried it—Ben said I was funny." That confidence opened doors.

Steps:
1. **Set up low-pressure playdates**—small, structured, short.
2. **Role-play social situations**: joining games, introducing themselves.
3. **Discuss friendship stories**: "How did that character feel?"
4. **Model empathy and just talk about feelings** at home often.
5. **Praise effort in connection**: "You tried again—that's brave."

Final Encouragement

There's no perfect script for raising boys. You just need presence, patience, and a plan that fits *your* child. Keep showing up. Keep learning together. And celebrate progress over perfection.

You're not alone—and your steady love is doing more than you can see.

Please Leave a 1-click Review!

I would be incredibly thankful if you could take just 60 seconds to write a brief review on the platform of purchase, even if it's just a few sentences!

Conclusion
Raising Boys with Purpose and Compassion

Raising a son is not just a task, it's also a calling. It's a sacred ground, a trust handed to you by God Himself. Starting from the very first sleepy newborn stretch to the wild energy of the pre-teen years, you are shaping not just a child, but the man that he will one day become. His future as a husband, father, leader—even how he relates to God—can begin with how you listen, hug, guide, and discipline today.

This isn't a straight road. It's a winding, messy, joy-drenched hike uphill—with moments when you'll feel like you're failing, and others when you'll glimpse the fruit of your faithful effort.

Real Story: From Tears to Trust

Let me tell you about Nicole, a mum of two boys who was once described as "yelling more than praying." Her mornings were very chaotic. Her youngest would scream over his socks. Her eldest—age 9—was shutting down emotionally. Then, she shifted. One night she sat on the edge of their bed and whispered a simple prayer: *"Lord, help me parent with peace."*

She added a 3-minute "Prayer and Plan" each night—hug, verse, one win, one goal. She began replacing yelling with questions like, *"What's happening in your heart right now?"* Within weeks, her boys were still loud—but connected, calmer. Her home didn't become perfect, but it became peaceful. Progress over perfection.

How to Make the Most of What You've Learned

You now have a real toolbox with emotional intelligence, discipline with love, spiritual rituals, mentoring frameworks, and age-specific cues that you can use. Here's how to make them work:

1. Build Emotional Trust

Children thrive where they feel emotionally very safe. That safety is built through:

- **Daily Check-Ins**: Ask at bedtime, "What made your heart feel heavy or happy today?"

- **Emotion Cards or Charts**: For younger boys—use emojis or faces to help name feelings.

- **Listening without Fixing**: Just pause, affirm, repeat what they said—*"So you're feeling angry because that felt unfair?"*

Biblical Insight: Think of **Jesus with children**—He didn't correct first; He welcomed first (Mark 10:14). He listened. He saw. Be that safe space.

2. Establish Age-Based Spiritual Routines

Here's a simple chart you can stick on the fridge or keep in your phone:

Age	Spiritual Habit	How It Works
0–2	"God Loves Me" song	Sing while dressing or bathing; ends with a kiss and hug.
3–5	Kindness Prayer	After play, ask: "What kind thing did you do today? Thank God for it."
6–8	Verse + Value	Weekly verse + "value of the week"—e.g., honesty or patience.
9–12	Reflection Sundays	Write 2 lines in a faith journal + chat about a biblical hero challenge.

Biblical Hero: Teach them about **David**—a boy who fought lions, wrote Psalms, and made mistakes but always returned to God. That kind of man is raised through rhythm, not rules.

3. Anchor Mentorship and Emotional Boundaries
- **Mentor Meal Moments**: Once a month, have a male mentor (dad, uncle, godfather, coach) share a meal and speak on courage, discipline, or faith.

- **Values Tracker**: Create a "Growth Wall"—track their weekly kindness, self-control, or honesty moments. Celebrate them.

- **Use Consequences with Grace**: Like the **Prodigal Father**, offer both correction and compassion. When your son returns after defiance—run to him, but also teach him why the journey mattered.

What Matters Most
Don't fear the hard days. Elijah wanted to give up too—he felt overwhelmed, exhausted, alone. But God didn't scold him. God gave him rest, food, and a quiet word (1 Kings 19). That's parenting, too. Sometimes your son's rebellion is actually fatigue, hunger, confusion—or just a test of trust. Meet him where he is. Gently. Firmly. Faithfully.

Trust the Process (Step by Step)
- **Pick One Routine to Start** this week—bedtime prayers, a "God-happy" story time, or a mentor check-in.

- **Be Consistent for 7 Days.** If you miss a day—reset, don't quit.

- **Celebrate Wins.** Use stickers, charts, high-fives, or quiet smiles. Let him know his heart matters.

- **Pray Together.** Before school, whisper a 10-second blessing: *"God, guide his words and heart today."*

- **Record One Thing You Learned** about your son each week. What's he afraid of? What's he excited about?

Final Blessing: Your Faithful Work Matters
You're not just packing lunches or correcting tantrums. You're forming a soul. You're not raising a boy—you're raising someone's future husband, someone's father, someone's leader. And in that <u>sacred work which you are doing,</u> heaven is cheering you on.

Let this truth carry you:
> "Train up a child in the way he should go, and when he is old, he will not depart from it." – ***Proverbs 22:6***

Your faithfulness, though it is very small as it sometimes feels, it does ripples into generations.

Thank you for choosing this very book, for investing in your son's heart and future. May God bless your efforts, multiply your wisdom, and give you deep joy on the days you least expect it.

Recommended Resource Pairing
Book: *The Child Development and Positive Parenting Master Class* by Bukky Ekine Ogunlana

Great for: conflict resolution tools, emotional coaching scripts, learning techniques for every stage—Pre-K through teen years.

Final Thought
This book is more than chapters—it's a rhythm. Return to it. Reread a section when you feel stuck. Try a new routine when the old one dries up. And know this:

Every verse whispered, every tantrum navigated with grace, every bedtime prayer—it's all building something eternal.

You're not just raising boys. You're raising legacy.

Other Books You'll Love!

1. The Fear of The Lord: How God's Honour Guarantees Your Peace
2. Parenting Teenage Girls for Purpose: Guiding Godly Young Girls to Walk in Charisma, Character, Calling, Life Skills, and Christ-Centered Confidence
3. Parenting Teenage Boys for Purpose: Guiding Godly Young Girls to Walk in Charisma, Character, Calling, Life Skills, and Christ-Centered Confidence
4. Raising Teenagers to Choose Wisely: Keeping your Teen Secure in a Big World
5. Spelling one: An Interactive Vocabulary & Spelling Workbook for 5-Year-Olds. *(With Audiobook Lessons)*
6. Spelling Two: An Interactive Vocabulary & Spelling Workbook for 6-Year-Olds. *(With Audiobook Lessons)*
7. Spelling Three: An Interactive Vocabulary & Spelling Workbook for 7-Year-Olds. *(With Audiobook Lessons)*
8. Spelling Four: An Interactive Vocabulary & Spelling Workbook for 8-Year-Olds. *(With Audiobook Lessons)*
9. Spelling Five: An Interactive Vocabulary & Spelling Workbook for 9-Year-Olds. *(With Audiobook Lessons)*
10. Spelling Six: An Interactive Vocabulary & Spelling Workbook for 10 & 11 Years Old. *(With Audiobook Lessons)*

11. Spelling Seven: An Interactive Vocabulary & Spelling Workbook for 12-14 Years-Old. *(With Audiobook Lessons)*

12. Raising Boys in Today's Digital World: Proven Positive Parenting Tips for Raising Respectful, Successful, and Confident Boys

13. Raising Girls in Today's Digital World: Proven Positive Parenting Tips for Raising Respectful, Successful, and Confident Girls

14. Raising Kids in Today's Digital World: Proven Positive Parenting Tips for Raising Respectful, Successful, and Confident Kids

15. The Child Development and Positive Parenting Master Class 2-in-1 Bundle: Proven Methods for Raising Well-Behaved and Intelligent Children, with Accelerated Learning Methods

16. Parenting Teens in Today's Challenging World 2-in-1 Bundle: Proven Methods for Improving Teenager's Behaviour with Positive Parenting and Family Communication

17. Life Strategies for Teenagers: Positive Parenting, Tips and Understanding Teens for Better Communication and a Happy Family

18. Parenting Teen Girls in Today's Challenging World: Proven Methods for Improving Teenager's Behaviour with Whole Brain Training

19. Parenting Teen Boys in Today's Challenging World: Proven Methods for Improving Teenager's Behaviour with Whole Brain Training

20. 101 Tips For Helping With Your Child's Learning: Proven Strategies for Accelerated Learning and Raising Smart Children Using Positive Parenting Skills

21. 101 Tips for Child Development: Proven Methods for Raising Children and Improving Kids Behavior with Whole Brain Training

22. Financial Tips to Help Kids: Proven Methods for Teaching Kids Money Management and Financial Responsibility

23. Healthy Habits for Kids: Positive Parenting Tips for Fun Kids Exercises, Healthy Snacks, and Improved Kids Nutrition

24. Mini Habits for Happy Kids: Proven Parenting Tips for Positive Discipline and Improving Kids' Behavior

25. Good Habits for Healthy Kids 2-in-1 Combo Pack: Proven Positive Parenting Tips for Improving Kid's Fitness and Children's Behavior

26. T Raising Teenagers to Choose Wisely: Keeping your Teen Secure in a Big World

27. Tips for #CollegeLife: Powerful College Advice for Excelling as a College Freshman

28. The Career Success Formula: Proven Career Development Advice and Finding Rewarding Employment for Young Adults and College Graduates

29. The Motivated Young Adult's Guide to Career Success and Adulthood: Proven Tips for Becoming a Mature Adult, Starting a Rewarding Career, and Finding Life Balance

30. Bedtime Stories for Kids: Short Funny Stories and poems Collection for Children and Toddlers

31. Guide for Boarding School Life

Facebook Community

I will like to invite you to our Facebook community group to visit this link and simply click the join group.

https://www.facebook.com/groups/397683731371863

This is a private group where parents, teachers, and carers can learn, share tips, ask questions, discuss and get valuable content about raising and parent modern children. It is a very supportive and encouraging group where valuable content, free resources, and exciting discussion about parenting are being shared. You can use this to benefit from social media. You will be learning a lot from school teachers, experts, counselors, new and experienced parents, and stay updated with our latest releases.

See you there!

References

[1] https://cchp.ucsf.edu/sites/g/files/tkssra181/f/SelfEsteem_en0710.pdf

[2] https://www.theseus.fi/bitstream/handle/10024/50239/Anttila_Marianna_Saikkonen_Pinja.pdf

[3] https://ijcat.com/archives/volume5/issue2/ijcatr05021006.pdf

[4] https://www.harvey.k-state.edu/family-and-consumer-sciences/family_and_child_development/documents/CommunicatingwTeenTrust.pdf

[5] https://www.researchgate.net/publication/283721084_Early_Reading_Development

[6] https://www.understood.org/en/friends-feelings/empowering-your-child/building-on-strengths/download-hands-on-activity-to-identify-your-childs-strengths

[7] https://www.wfm.noaa.gov/pdfs/ParentingYourTeen_Handout1.pdf

[8] https://www.helpguide.org/articles/depression/parents-guide-to-teen-depression.htm?pdf=13027

[9] https://www2.ed.gov/parents/academic/help/adolescence/adolescence.pdf

[10] http://centerforchildwelfare.org/kb/prprouthome/Helping%20Your%20Children%20Navigate%20Their%20Teenage%20Years.pdf

[11] https://www.childrensmn.org/images/family_resource_pdf/027121.pdf

[12] https://educationnorthwest.org/sites/default/files/developing-empathy-in-children-and-youth.pdf

[13] http://drkateaubrey.com/wp-content/uploads/2016/02/Parenting-Your-Strong-Willed-Child.pdf

[14] https://www.researchgate.net/publication/263227023_Family_Time_Activities_and_Adolescents'_Emotional_Well-being

[15] https://parenting-ed.org/wp-content/themes/parenting-ed/files/handouts/communication-parent-to-child.pdf

[16] https://www.wikihow.mom/Trust-Your-Teenager

[17] https://www.statmodel.com/download/Meeus,%20vd%20Schoot,%20Klimstra%20&.pdf

[18] https://www.nap.edu/resource/19401/ProfKnowCompFINAL.pdf

[19] http://www.delmarlearning.com/companions/content/1418019224/AdditionalSupport/box11.1.pdf

[20] http://resources.beyondblue.org.au/prism/file?token=BL/1810_A

[21] https://exeter.anglican.org/wp-content/uploads/2014/11/Listening-to-children-leaflet_NCB.pdf

[22] https://www.researchgate.net/publication/312600262_Creative_Thinking_among_Preschool_Children

[23] https://www.gutenberg.org/files/15114/15114-pdf.pdf

[24] https://discovery.ucl.ac.uk/id/eprint/1522668/1/Thesis%20Moulton%20V%20281016.pdf

[25] https://www.bda.uk.com/foodfacts/healthyeatingchildren.pdf

[26] http://www.tuskmont.org/uploads/1/7/7/2/17728377/follow_the_child_trust_the_child.pdf

[27] https://www.apa.org/pi/families/resources/develop.pdf

[28] https://extension.colostate.edu/docs/pubs/consumer/10249.pdf

[29] https://www.empoweringparents.com/article/risky-teen-behavior-can-you-trust-your-child-again/

[30] http://www.wecf.eu/download/2018/05%20May/WSSPPublicationENPartC-MHMchapter.pdf

www.ingramcontent.com/pod-product-compliance
Lightning Source LLC
Chambersburg PA
CBHW071531080526
44588CB00011B/1633